MW01487503

Original title:
Where Dreams Wear Smiles

Author: Aron Pilviste
ISBN HARDBACK: 978-9908-1-4441-2
ISBN PAPERBACK: 978-9908-1-4442-9
ISBN EBOOK: 978-9908-1-4443-6

The Language of Merry Secrets

In whispers soft, the night confides,
The stars align where laughter hides.
Beneath the moon, we share our dreams,
In gentle tones, or so it seems.

With every glance, a secret grows,
In twilight's veil, the magic flows.
Our hearts converse in silent waves,
Painting tales the heart enslaves.

In every smile, a world awakes,
As fleeting moments softly break.
We weave our paths in colors bright,
In shadows deep, our souls take flight.

Just like the breeze that bends the leaves,
We find the truth that quietly weaves.
Through laughter's glow and whispered sighs,
The language shared beneath the skies.

And in this dance, we understand,
The merry secrets hand in hand.
As stars will fade and dawn will rise,
Our stories live in endless ties.

The Radiance of Beaming Hopes

In the dawn's embrace, dreams take flight,
Golden rays dance, igniting the night.
Whispers of joy, in every heart found,
With courage we rise, from the soft ground.

Every step forward, with love as our guide,
Through valleys of doubt, we boldly stride.
A symphony sings of a future so bright,
In the glow of hope, we bask in the light.

Reflections in a Laughter-Laden Lake

Ripples of laughter, under a blue sky,
Echoing moments that swiftly glide by.
Children at play, with innocence pure,
In the shimmering water, memories endure.

The sun dips low, painting colors so bold,
With tales of joy in the twilight told.
Mirrored reflections of smiles so wide,
In nature's embrace, we forever abide.

The Secret Garden of Happy Hours

Hidden away, where the wildflowers grow,
A sanctuary blooms, with beauty in tow.
Whispers of petals, secrets they share,
In the garden of time, we breathe in the air.

Each moment a treasure, each laugh a refrain,
In the warmth of togetherness, we dance in the rain.
Beneath leafy canopies, joy finds its place,
In the secret garden, we savor each grace.

Whimsical Wonders in Shimmering Realms

In lands where dreams twirl in the breeze,
Magic and wonder weave through the trees.
Stars wink and giggle, in a playful dance,
Inviting our hearts to join in the chance.

With every adventure, new stories unfold,
In shimmering realms, where dreams are retold.
Where the oddities roam, and laughter ignites,
In whimsical wonders, we chase through the nights.

Serenade of Listen and Laugh

In twilight's glow, whispers play,
Laughter dances, lighting the way.
Softly we share the tales of old,
Echoes of joy, heartaches retold.

Together we weave a melody sweet,
Each note a treasure, a cherished defeat.
With every chuckle, our souls entwine,
In this sweet serenade, life feels divine.

Fantasies Wrapped in Sunbeams

Chasing horizons where dreams ignite,
Sunbeams wrap us in warm delight.
In gardens of wonder, wildflowers bloom,
Each petal a whisper, dispelling the gloom.

A canvas of colors, so vivid, so bright,
Imaginations soar, taking flight.
With every glance, the world shifts and sways,
Fantasies woven, igniting our days.

The Enchanted Smile Escape

A smile, a treasure, a beacon of light,
In shadowy corners, it shines ever bright.
Together we wander, hearts open wide,
In laughter and joy, our worries subside.

Magic unfolds in the simplest ways,
With glimmers of hope that forever stay.
In this enchanted realm, we find our place,
Forever embraced in a warm, loving space.

Flickers of Light in Darkened Days

When shadows loom and silence grows,
Flickers of light, the spirit knows.
In moments of doubt, a spark will appear,
Guiding us gently, dispelling our fear.

Each flicker, a promise, a reason to fight,
Illuminating paths through the long, dark night.
Together we stand, hand in hand, ablaze,
Finding our strength in those flickering rays.

Reflections in a Pool of Joy

In the stillness, laughter rings,
Ripples dance with the joy it brings.
Sunlight winks on the surface bright,
Every moment, a sheer delight.

Flecks of color, a vibrant glow,
In the water, soft whispers flow.
Dreams like pebbles, gently tossed,
In every splash, no thought of loss.

Mirrors of the heart so clear,
Capturing wishes, banishing fear.
Bubbles rise like hopes set free,
In this pool, I find the real me.

Soft reflections of days gone by,
Memories shimmer, flutter, and fly.
A cradle of peace, I find within,
In this joy, new journeys begin.

Every glance brings a smile anew,
Life's pure essence, a brilliant hue.
In each splash, a story unfolds,
In the pool of joy, life's wonder holds.

The Palette of Euphoric Visions

Colors swirl in a painter's dream,
Vivid hues in a radiant stream.
Strokes of passion, every glance,
In this canvas, our spirits dance.

Golden sunbeams, a warm embrace,
Whispers of magic, fill the space.
With every shade, a tale is spun,
Beneath the sky, we laugh and run.

Tulip fields stretch far and wide,
Nature's masterpiece, a joyous ride.
Crimson skies at dusk's soft call,
In this palette, we find our all.

Every brushstroke, a heartbeat's sigh,
Capturing moments that never die.
Within the spectrum, love's sweet kiss,
In euphoric visions, we find bliss.

Through vibrant tones, our souls ignite,
In colors rich, we take our flight.
With every hue, a new path starts,
In this palette, we share our hearts.

Blossoms of Hope in Brightness

In the garden where dreams take root,
Petals unfurl, a tender fruit.
Colors awaken in morning light,
Each blossom whispers, hope takes flight.

Dewdrops glisten like gems of sighs,
Fragile moments beneath the skies.
With every breeze, sweet scents combine,
In this haven, all hearts align.

Sun-kissed blooms rise from the ground,
Hope's gentle laughter all around.
Every blossom tells a story,
In nature's realm, we find our glory.

Among the petals, hues so bright,
Casting shadows, chasing the night.
In the fragrance, memories dwell,
In each blossom, a wish to tell.

With every season, cycles renew,
In each blossom, the promise is true.
Hope unfurls in gentle embrace,
In the brightness, we find our place.

Portraits of Delightful Wanderlust

Paths that twist through valleys wide,
Adventurers' hearts, forever tied.
Mountains echo our laughter clear,
In every journey, love draws near.

From city lights to tranquil shores,
Each moment opens hidden doors.
With every step, the world expands,
In wanderlust, we take our stands.

Fields of gold under boundless skies,
With curious eyes, we seek the prize.
The rhythm of places intertwined,
In exploration, our hearts aligned.

With every sunrise, new tales unfold,
Windows to wonders waiting untold.
For in each corner of land and sea,
Delightful wanderlust sets us free.

Frames of happiness in every place,
Stories written on nature's face.
Together we roam, hand in hand,
In these portraits, forever we stand.

A Hidden Path of Gentle Laughter

In the woods where shadows play,
A hidden path winds soft and gay.
Whispers dance on the cool breeze,
Carried forth by ancient trees.

Footsteps tickle the ground with glee,
Where laughter echoes wild and free.
Sunbeams filter through the leaves,
Painting magic as the heart believes.

Gentle streams weave through the glade,
Reflecting dreams that never fade.
Petals float on a silver brook,
Inviting all to stop and look.

Beneath the boughs, hearts intertwine,
Moments linger, pure and divine.
In laughter's embrace, we find our way,
On a hidden path, we choose to stay.

Melodies of Laughter Across the Horizon

Under a sky painted in blue,
Melodies of laughter flow anew.
Across the fields, like a sweet breeze,
They dance and swirl with effortless ease.

Echoes rise with the sun's warm glow,
In the golden light, joy starts to grow.
Children play where wildflowers sway,
Creating tunes that brighten the day.

As twilight falls, the stars appear,
Laughter lingers, soft and clear.
Each note carried on the night air,
A symphony of love and care.

Horizon blushes in shades of gold,
With stories of laughter yet untold.
In its embrace, our spirits soar,
Uniting hearts forevermore.

The Bloom of Elysian Whispers

In gardens where the wild winds sigh,
Elysian whispers softly lie.
Petals brush against the soul,
In their presence, we feel whole.

Each bloom a secret, bright and sweet,
Offers comfort where hearts meet.
The fragrance twirls through the air,
Caressing dreams, gentle and rare.

Underneath the arching trees,
Time stands still as we find ease.
Moments linger like a tender kiss,
In this realm of purest bliss.

Whispers echo in the night,
Guiding us toward the light.
With every step, we start to see,
The beauty of what's meant to be.

Sun-kissed Reveries of Joyous Nights

As daylight fades, the stars awake,
Sun-kissed reveries begin to take.
Around the fire, stories blend,
Of laughter shared with every friend.

In the warmth of twilight's embrace,
Joyous nights find their sacred space.
With music floating on the breeze,
Hearts unite with effortless ease.

Moonbeams dance on the gentle waves,
Whispers of joy that the heart saves.
Each moment shared beneath the sky,
Transforms the world, makes spirits fly.

As night unfolds its velvet cloak,
Dreams awaken, laughter spoke.
In these hours, we truly find,
The sun-kissed memories intertwined.

Whispers of Joyful Fantasies

In the hush of twilight's glow,
Dreams take flight on wings of gold.
Each whisper soft, a tale to tell,
Of joys that in our hearts unfold.

In fields where laughter lightly spills,
Children dance beneath the trees.
Their playful giggles drift like air,
Carried forth by the gentle breeze.

Stars awaken, twinkling bright,
Guiding hopes through night's embrace.
In the silence, hearts unite,
Finding peace in dreams' sweet space.

Softly glows a vibrant hue,
With every thought, a song is spun.
In joyful realms, we wander free,
Together 'til the night is done.

From shadows rise the brightest beams,
Unraveled threads of love and light.
In whispers wrapped in endless dreams,
We find our way through dark to bright.

Laughter in a Moonlit Reverie

Beneath the moon's enchanting gaze,
Laughter dances in the night.
Every echo brings a smile,
In the soft, silver light.

Whispers weave through misty air,
As shadows play, their secrets shared.
Time stands still in this sweet dream,
In a world of joy, unprepared.

The nightingale sings a tune so sweet,
In the heart of this magical hour.
Stars above in twilight greet,
As dreams unfold, like blooming flower.

Together we find, in every sigh,
The essence of love's gentle grace.
In laughter, we learn to fly,
In the moonlit reverie's embrace.

With every heartbeat, moments last,
Layered memories softly blend.
In shadows cast by light so vast,
We hold tight, our dreams ascend.

The Garden of Glowing Visions

In a garden where colors bloom,
Visions glimmer in the dawn.
Every petal whispers dreams,
In the light, our hopes are drawn.

Softly sways the fragrant breeze,
Carrying secrets, wild and true.
In this haven, love's at ease,
Woven in the morning dew.

Butterflies drift, a ballet sweet,
Painting joy with wings of grace.
In this space, we find our beat,
As nature wraps us in its embrace.

Voices mingle, a lively song,
With laughter echoing so bright.
Here where every heart belongs,
We dance together, pure delight.

As the sun begins to rise,
Hope awakes with every hue.
In this garden full of sighs,
We nurture dreams, and visions bloom.

Echoes of Cheerful Aspirations

In the heart of every dream,
Lies the spark of bright desire.
Echoes ring, a joyful theme,
Fueling souls with passion's fire.

Every hope a shining star,
Guiding paths through dark and light.
With each step, we journey far,
Chasing visions, hearts take flight.

The laughter shared in moments brief,
Paints the canvas of our days.
In every sorrow, find relief,
For joy blooms in the sweetest ways.

Together we rise, hand in hand,
With dreams that sway like trees above.
In this life, a vibrant band,
Echoes dance in endless love.

With every heartbeat, aspirations soar,
We carve our names in skies wide-flung.
In cheerful notes, our spirits roar,
Echoing the song of youth, still sung.

Pathways Painted in Joy

Through sunlit streets we roam,
With laughter echoing loud.
Every step a dance we share,
In this vibrant, living crowd.

Colors burst like blooming flowers,
In the air their fragrance sways.
Joyful hearts in rhythm beat,
Guiding us through endless days.

We trace the lines of friendship's grace,
Each moment, a thread we weave.
Together we build our dreams,
In this tapestry we believe.

A canvas rich with loving hues,
As time slips past like sand.
Every smile a brushstroke bright,
Painted by a grateful hand.

So let us wander hand in hand,
In pathways painted so bright.
With every step, we choose to laugh,
Spreading joy like morning light.

The Canvas of Bittersweet Laughter

In a world of ups and downs,
A smile hides a tear,
We paint our lives in shades of love,
While wrestling with our fear.

Brush of sadness softly strokes,
Blending warm with cold,
Each moment holds a story told,
In colors bright and bold.

Echoes of laughter waltz through pain,
Creating melodies sweet.
We find the beauty in the cracks,
In losses, we dare to meet.

Yet in this vibrant tapestry,
Bittersweet moments bloom.
We celebrate the fleeting time,
As shadows fill the room.

So let us hold this precious blend,
Of laughter and of sighs.
For in the dance of joy and ache,
True beauty never dies.

Melodies of Hope and Radiance

In the whisper of the dawn,
Hope sings through the trees.
Each note a promise carried forth,
Riding on the breeze.

Radiance spills from golden skies,
Chasing shadows away.
With every heartbeat, we feel alive,
Welcoming the new day.

Harmony flows like a gentle stream,
Washing worries aside.
Melodies of dreams take flight,
On wings of joy, we ride.

In this symphony of light,
We gather strength anew.
Together we create the sounds,
That echo hope so true.

So let us sing in unison,
With voices bold and free.
For in the melodies we share,
We find our unity.

Silhouettes of Grinning Dreams

At twilight's touch, shadows rise,
Silhouettes on the wall.
With grinning dreams that dance and swirl,
In twilight's gentle call.

Fleeting figures glide with grace,
Each one a laughing face.
In the stillness of the night,
We find our dreamer's space.

They whisper tales of distant lands,
Where wishes bloom and soar.
With every leap, they chase the stars,
And seek forevermore.

Together, we embrace the night,
In a world of whispered schemes.
For in the dark, our hopes take flight,
As we weave our grinning dreams.

So let the shadows lead the way,
And fill our hearts with cheer.
In silhouettes of joy we find,
Our aspirations clear.

A Kaleidoscope of Happy Endings

In the light of dawn, dreams take flight,
Colors twirl, painting futures bright.
Every moment, a chance to mend,
A dance of joy, where hearts transcend.

Laughter echoes in the gentle breeze,
Filling the air with sweet memories.
With every step, we find our way,
In this kaleidoscope, night turns to day.

Bridges built from love's pure thread,
Each new path, bravely we tread.
Hand in hand, we shall explore,
The magic of life, forevermore.

Stars align in a cosmic smile,
Guiding our souls across each mile.
With every twist, new tales to share,
In this vibrant world, we find our flair.

So raise a glass to the dreams we've spun,
To the battles fought and the victories won.
In every ending, a spark we send,
A kaleidoscope of hope, our hearts' blend.

Charms of Uplifting Whispers

Whispers of hope dance on the air,
Carried softly, like a gentle prayer.
Each secret shared, a treasure rare,
Woven with love, beyond compare.

Sunlight glimmers on the dew-kissed grass,
Every moment fragile, yet a joy to pass.
With every heartbeat, we choose to rise,
Embracing laughter that energizes.

In the canvas of a vibrant sky,
Brilliant hues blend, as hopes fly high.
We paint our stories, vivid and bright,
Creating a symphony, pure delight.

With every word, the spirit soars,
Unlocking dreams behind closed doors.
A melody soft, an uplifting tune,
Guiding us gently, like the light of the moon.

So listen closely to the charms around,
In every whisper, pure joy is found.
With open hearts, let our spirits gleam,
In the embrace of love, we dare to dream.

The Flicker of a Hopeful Heart

A spark ignites in the silent night,
With every breath, we chase the light.
In shadows deep, a promise gleams,
A flicker of hope within our dreams.

Stars twinkle like wishes on display,
Guiding us gently along the way.
Through trials faced, courage we find,
With every heartbeat, love intertwined.

A beacon shines when the world feels cold,
A story of strength ready to be told.
In the warmth of friendship, we rise above,
Nurtured by kindness, wrapped in love.

Though storms may rage, hearts stand tall,
United we rise, we'll never fall.
In the flicker, we discover art,
The beautiful dance of a hopeful heart.

So hold on tight to the dreams we weave,
In every moment, dare to believe.
With every flicker, let our spirits soar,
Together we'll shine, forevermore.

Harmony in a Smiling Universe

Under the vast sky, stars align,
In every heartbeat, a gentle sign.
With laughter ringing, we're never alone,
In this smiling universe, love is sown.

Planets spin in a cosmic ballet,
Moving together, come what may.
Each twinkle whispers secrets untold,
The beauty of life, unyielding and bold.

Every smile shared is a beacon bright,
Turning the dark into glorious light.
With every step on this radiant ground,
Harmony sings in the joy we've found.

Embracing each moment with open arms,
In a world filled with wonder and charms.
Together we rise, forever we'll sing,
In this universe, let our hearts take wing.

So cherish the day and the night's delight,
In the tapestry woven from joy and light.
For in every heartbeat, we hold the key,
To harmony's song in life's symphony.

Crescendos of Playful Clouds

Soft whispers roll in skies,
Gentle hues in playful guise.
Bonds of light, they twist and twine,
Over fields where dreams align.

Laughter dances on the breeze,
Carried high with playful ease.
Fluttering wings from creatures small,
Echo joy, their voices call.

Shadows play amidst the day,
As the sun leads them away.
A tapestry of white and blue,
Each moment bright, if tried and true.

Through the air, a silent song,
Where the happy wanderers long.
Weaving tales, both bright and bold,
In the skies where joys unfold.

Journeying Through Delightful Landscapes

Footsteps crunch on paths of gold,
Nature's wonders, joys unfold.
Meadows sway with colors bright,
Guiding hearts toward pure delight.

Mountains rise with gentle grace,
Inviting us to roam and chase.
Rivers sing with playful glee,
Whispers carried from the sea.

Every turn reveals a scene,
A painted world of lush green sheen.
Stars above in twilight kiss,
Mark the journey's tranquil bliss.

Bridges span o'er valleys wide,
Each step taken with hearts full of pride.
The map of joy lies in the heart,
In every path, a brand new start.

The Playful Song of Carefree Hearts

In a field where laughter flies,
Children chase beneath the skies.
With open arms, they spin around,
As giggles form a joyous sound.

Sunshine wraps the day in cheer,
Every moment held so dear.
Swinging high, the world's a blur,
In their hearts, sweet dreams confer.

Dancing shadows round the trees,
Rustling leaves and gentle breeze.
A playful song, a heart's delight,
Weaving magic through the night.

With every step, a story made,
In the dusk, no fears invade.
Carefree spirits, free and wild,
Life is sweet, forever styled.

Canvas of Joy in the Midnight Hour

Stars emerge, the night is deep,
In silence, dreams begin to leap.
Canvas drawn with strokes of light,
Whispers weave through velvet night.

Moonbeams paint the world in gold,
Stories waiting to be told.
Echoes of a distant song,
Calling souls to dance along.

Fireflies blink, like tiny sparks,
Mapping paths through hidden parks.
Joy spills out beneath the sky,
As dreams take form and gently fly.

Together we share this hour,
In perfect peace, in love's great power.
Breathe it in, the night is kind,
A canvas bright, our hearts combined.

Tales of Gleeful Solitude

In a quiet nook of time,
A single leaf falls free,
Whispers dance with glee,
As shadows skip with me.

Beneath the ancient trees,
A laughter never heard,
The breeze hums soft and low,
In this blissful world.

Stars twinkle in the night,
With secrets on their lips,
The moon a silent guide,
In solitude's sweet grip.

Each thought a painted brush,
Colors swirl in my mind,
Dreams of endless wonder,
In tranquil moments find.

Here, the heart takes flight,
In realms of quiet song,
The tales of gleeful days,
Where I truly belong.

Chasing Sunsets with Grinning Souls

On painted skies of gold,
We run with hearts aglow,
Laughter rings like bells,
As the soft winds blow.

Through fields of wildflowers,
Our spirits dance and soar,
Chasing sunlit wonders,
Counting joys and more.

Each sunset paints a story,
Of days we won't forget,
With grinning souls beside,
In dreams we won't regret.

We sketch in azure skies,
Moments pure and bright,
Hand in hand we wander,
Into the velvet night.

Every dusk we treasure,
As we twirl and spin,
Chasing sunsets endlessly,
Where our hearts begin.

The Happy Echo of Silent Wishes

In the stillness of the dawn,
Wishes float like dreams,
Softly echoing through time,
In the morning's beams.

A whisper in the breeze,
Carries hopes held near,
Silent wishes drift away,
With each drop of tear.

In the corners of the heart,
Joy and sorrow blend,
A happy echo rings out,
As we start to mend.

With every fleeting thought,
A chance to break the chains,
Finding strength in silence,
Where love forever reigns.

These wishes, like soft lights,
Guide us through the dark,
Radiant and gentle,
They ignite a spark.

Unraveled Curiosities of Sea-Salted Joy

On sandy shores I wander,
With waves that kiss my feet,
The salt of earth and ocean,
In every breath I meet.

Curiosities unfold,
In shells that tell a tale,
Of hidden worlds beneath,
Where dreams set sail.

The wind carries my laughter,
As whispers blend with foam,
Each grain of sand a story,
In this heartfelt home.

I gather bits of wonder,
From tides that ebb and flow,
Unraveled joys abound,
In the moon's soft glow.

Here, where the sun meets sea,
In joy that's ever clear,
I find my sacred space,
Where every day is dear.

Portraits of Blissful Wishes

In gardens where lilies sway,
Whispers of hope gently play.
Dreams unbridled, taking flight,
Painting joy in morning light.

Gentle breezes carry tales,
Of distant shores and lovely gales.
Every wish, a seed that's sown,
In fields of love, forever grown.

Butterflies dance on sunlit streams,
Chasing softly woven dreams.
Each moment, a treasure rare,
A canvas bright, beyond compare.

With laughter ringing through the air,
A symphony of hearts laid bare.
In harmony, we find our truth,
The fleeting grace of endless youth.

So let us raise our voices high,
Embracing life, we dare to fly.
For every wish, a chance to be,
A portrait drawn of blissful glee.

Celestial Laughs and Starlit Paths

Underneath the velvet night,
Stars are winking, pure delight.
Galaxies weave a cosmic dance,
Inviting hearts to take a chance.

Moonbeams glow, a silver thread,
Guiding dreams as softly said.
Each twinkle holds a playful joke,
In shared laughs, our spirits woke.

Lost in awe, we wander free,
Tracing trails of destiny.
With every step, a story spun,
Celestial laughs, the journey's fun.

Beneath the vast and endless skies,
We find our truth in clever lies.
The paths we take, forever dear,
With starlit joy that draws us near.

As shadows fade to dawn's first light,
We cherish nights that felt so right.
In laughter's embrace, we will tread,
On starlit paths where dreams are fed.

The Melody of Joyful Musings

Softly hums the morning breeze,
Carrying notes among the trees.
A melody of sweet delight,
Awakens hearts to morning light.

With every song, a tale unfolds,
As whispers of the dawn retold.
Joyful musings dance in air,
In every glance, a fleeting prayer.

The laughter of the streams below,
Plays a rhythm, soft and low.
Every bird that takes to flight,
Sings of dreams, pure and bright.

In nature's choir, we find our voice,
In harmony, we make our choice.
To revel in the fleeting rays,
Of life's sweet yet bittersweet plays.

So let us join this merry tune,
Beneath the sun, the stars, the moon.
For in this dance, our spirits soar,
A melody we can't ignore.

Dancing Shadows of Delight

When twilight drapes the world in grace,
Shadows twirl at a gentle pace.
In every corner, laughter blooms,
As sunlight fades and evening looms.

The dance of night, a soft embrace,
Brings warmth to every hidden space.
In fleeting moments, joy ignites,
As shadows weave with starry lights.

Each flicker tells a tale anew,
Of dreams revisited, bright and true.
In twilight's glow, we lose all fears,
And find delight through laughter's tears.

Beneath the stars, we sway and spin,
With every heartbeat, we begin.
A waltz of hearts in perfect time,
To rhythms low, a sweet sublime.

So let us dance 'neath moonlit skies,
With open hearts and hopeful sighs.
For in these shadows, light will shine,
In every step, your hand in mine.

A Tapestry of Hopeful Dreams

In the quiet night, stars gleam bright,
Whispers of wishes take their flight.
Threads of hope weave through the air,
Painting visions beyond compare.

A canvas rich with colors bold,
Tales of futures yet untold.
Each stitch a promise, strong and true,
A tapestry of dreams anew.

With every dawn, the light breaks free,
Embracing life and possibility.
Every heartbeat, a rhythm sweet,
In this journey, we find our feet.

Through the storms, we will stay brave,
In the waters, we learn to wave.
Gathering strength from each setback,
Never once did we lose track.

So, we rise with the morning sun,
With every heartbeat, we have won.
A tapestry of hope, we weave,
In the dreams we dare to believe.

Hues of Laughter in Twilight

As the sun dips, colors blend,
Laughter dances, shadows extend.
Hues of joy paint the evening sky,
A chorus of giggles, oh so spry.

In the twilight, magic unfolds,
Stories of friendship gently told.
Soft whispers weave in the air,
Bonds of love, beyond compare.

With every star that begins to shine,
Connections deepen, hearts entwine.
Twilight's brush strokes, warm and bright,
Creating memories, pure delight.

Let the moonlight be our guide,
In this moment, let joy abide.
With every laugh, a spark ignites,
Painting our world with endless sights.

In the night's embrace, we take flight,
Carried by dreams that feel so right.
Hues of laughter forever sway,
In the twilight, we choose to play.

The Glow of Happy Horizons

Morning breaks with a golden hue,
A canvas fresh, alive, and new.
Horizons glow with endless cheer,
Inviting us to draw near.

Each sunrise whispers hope and grace,
In every heart, it finds a place.
With open arms, we greet the day,
Chasing worries far away.

Candles of passion light our way,
In the promise of a brighter day.
Moments gathered, stories shared,
In this journey, we are dared.

With every step, we feel alive,
In this world, we thrive and strive.
The glow of dreams shines ever bright,
Guiding us through the darkest night.

So let our spirits soar and roam,
In the warmth, we find our home.
The horizon calls with endless grace,
In this glow, we find our place.

Vibrant Smiles in the Clouds

Above the world, where dreams drift high,
Vibrant smiles in the clouds, we fly.
With every giggle, life unfolds,
A tapestry woven in bright golds.

In the breeze, laughter echoes clear,
Whispers of joy that we hold dear.
Each sunny ray, a playful tease,
Bringing warmth like a gentle breeze.

As we dance on a canvas vast,
Cherishing moments, holding fast.
Clouds parade, a whimsical view,
In this sky, life feels brand new.

With every change, colors embrace,
Strokes of happiness, joy's sweet chase.
In the shadows, we find the light,
Vibrant smiles, our hearts take flight.

So let us laugh, let our spirits soar,
In this journey, we ask for more.
Vibrant smiles, together we rise,
Painting our dreams across the skies.

Stars That Shine with Pure Smiles

In the night sky they gleam bright,
Whispering dreams in soft flight.
Each twinkle, a story untold,
Casting warmth, defying the cold.

Guiding souls with their light,
Filling hearts with pure delight.
They dance in the velvet sea,
Reminding us of what can be.

With every flicker, hope ignites,
In the shadows, they shine bright.
Stars that smile, pure and true,
Carrying wishes just for you.

A canvas of dreams above,
A testament to endless love.
Glistening gems in the night,
Holding secrets, shining bright.

As they fade with the dawn's ray,
Their promise lingers, come what may.
In our hearts, they remain still,
Stars that guide with gentle will.

The Brighter Side of Midnight

When the world is draped in dark,
Whispers of hope leave their mark.
In shadows dance the hopes unseen,
A canvas vibrant, serene.

Midnight holds a secret glow,
Where dreams and freedom ebb and flow.
Beyond the silence, life awaits,
Unlocking all the hidden gates.

Underneath the moon's soft glow,
The heart understands what it knows.
Memories twinkle like stars above,
In this stillness, we find love.

The clock strikes twelve, spirits rise,
Chasing dreams that never die.
With every breath, we take our flight,
Embracing joy, a pure delight.

Amid the hush, let laughter swell,
As midnight casts its magic spell.
We dance on the brighter side,
With open hearts, our hopes abide.

Radiant Wishes at Dawn's Embrace

The dawn breaks with colors bright,
A canvas painted with pure light.
Wishes ride the morning breeze,
Carried forth among the trees.

As sunlight spills across the sky,
We lift our voices, letting fly.
Radiant hopes in each heartbeat,
With every step, we feel complete.

Dew-kissed petals bathe the ground,
In every corner, joy is found.
The world awakens with a sigh,
As dreams unfold and spirits fly.

With every ray that warms the day,
We cast our doubts and fears away.
In dawn's embrace, we find our way,
Radiant wishes here to stay.

Moments linger, sweet and true,
In the light, we're born anew.
A tapestry of love and cheer,
Woven closely, year to year.

A Symphony of Contented Hearts

Together in this place we stand,
Creating music, hand in hand.
With every note, our souls align,
A symphony, sweet and divine.

In laughter's chorus, we find our song,
Echoing where we belong.
Heartbeats dance to a gentle tune,
Beneath the stars, under the moon.

Melodies of love fill the air,
Binding us in joy we share.
With each whisper, hope takes flight,
Guiding us through day and night.

The rhythm sways, a tender grace,
Every moment, a warm embrace.
Contentment flows in every part,
As harmony beats in every heart.

Together, we create our tale,
In this symphony, we shall sail.
Hand in hand, forever free,
A melody of you and me.

Unwritten Pages of Cheerful Mornings

The sun peeks through the curtain seams,
Awakening dreams in soft golden beams.
Birds chirp sweetly in the fresh dawn light,
A canvas awaits, each moment so bright.

Coffee brews with a fragrant delight,
As laughter rises to meet the day's height.
Whispers of joy in the breeze's embrace,
Unwritten pages, a sacred space.

Children gather in the garden's green,
Playing and laughing, a beautiful scene.
Nature joins in with a vibrant cheer,
Echoes of innocence pure and clear.

Each moment passes, a treasure to hold,
Stories of love in the hearts of the bold.
With every sunrise, fresh tales unfold,
Adventures waiting, as life will be told.

At twilight's fall, with colors ablaze,
We pen our stories in twilight's soft haze.
The cheerful mornings, forever we'll keep,
In the book of our hearts, where memories sleep.

Echoes of Laughter Beneath the Stars

Beneath the canvas of a midnight sky,
Moonlit whispers in the ether sigh.
Friends gather round with stories to share,
Echoes of laughter dancing in the air.

Stars twinkle bright, like secrets of old,
Tales of adventure in the night retold.
Fragrant breezes carry songs that we weave,
In the warmth of this night, we truly believe.

Moments flicker like fireflies in flight,
Every grin captured in the hush of the night.
Time stands still as we stand side by side,
In the glow of these memories, our hearts abide.

The world fades away, just a glimmering dream,
Lost in the joy of our radiant theme.
Hand in hand, we chase shadows afar,
Finding ourselves beneath the same star.

With each burst of laughter, our spirits will soar,
Echoes of happiness, forevermore.
Together we'll laugh, together we'll gleam,
And live this life, as a boundless dream.

The Fable of Blissful Sojourns

In lands of wonder, where stories unfold,
The fable of blissful sojourns is told.
Colors awaken in valleys so bright,
Where dreams take flight on the wings of the night.

Whispers of travelers, soft like the breeze,
Carry their laughter through shimmering trees.
In every step lies a journey not planned,
A tapestry woven by the traveler's hand.

Mountain peaks call with a promise so clear,
Each challenge faced, a moment to cheer.
Rivers of wisdom flow deep in our hearts,
And through every struggle, the magic imparts.

Sunset embraces the world in its fold,
Casting long shadows as tales are retold.
With friends by our side, adventure defined,
In the fable of travels, our souls intertwined.

Home is a feeling, wherever we roam,
In the joy of the journey, we've found our home.
Blissful sojourns, a lifetime we crave,
In every heartbeat, our spirits are brave.

Dances Beneath a Radiant Sky

When the sun dips low and the stars ignite,
We gather together to dance in the night.
Movements like petals, gentle and free,
In harmony swaying with each gentle breeze.

The moon casts a glow on our spirits so bright,
Embracing the rhythm, we sway in delight.
Feet finding joy on the soft, dewy grass,
Each twirl a reminder of moments that pass.

Laughter erupts like a sweet, bubbling stream,
Intertwined with music, we live in a dream.
As shadows grow longer and whispers engage,
We pen our own story upon life's grand stage.

Time slows its pace, as we twirl and spin,
With each fragile heartbeat, new memories begin.
Under the cosmos, our worries take flight,
In this dance of life, we embrace the night.

With spirits alight, we embrace the unknown,
Each twinkling star a key to our own.
Dances beneath this radiant sky,
Forever we'll cherish, as moments fly by.

Echoes of Joyful Whispers

In gardens where the lilies sway,
Soft voices linger, bright and play.
Laughter flutters on the breeze,
A melody that charms the trees.

Sun-kissed paths where shadows dance,
In every glance, a sweet romance.
Step by step, hearts beat as one,
In whispers shared, the day is won.

Through gentle winds, secrets unfold,
Stories of love in hues of gold.
Underneath the starry skies,
Joyful echoes never die.

Each moment held, a treasure rare,
In silent awe, we breathe the air.
Together here, we find our song,
In echoes of joy, we all belong.

Beneath the moon, the night beguiles,
As laughter travels countless miles.
In every sigh, there's magic spun,
Echoes of joy will never shun.

The Fabric of Laughter

We weave our dreams with threads of cheer,
In every stitch, we draw you near.
Colors bright, with stories spun,
Laughter ties us, two as one.

Soft embraces, comfort found,
In every giggle, love unwound.
Woven moments, warm and bright,
The fabric glows with pure delight.

Through whimsical tales and playful jest,
In tangled yarns, we find our rest.
A tapestry of joy's embrace,
Every smile, a cherished trace.

In patches sewn from time and care,
Laughter lingers, light as air.
Each thread a memory, sewn so tight,
In laughter's quilt, we find our light.

As time unfolds, our stories grow,
The fabric flows with vibrant glow.
In every chuckle, joy will last,
A tapestry of love amassed.

Hideaways in a Sunbeam

In golden rays where shadows play,
We find our hideaways each day.
Underneath the willow's sigh,
Cocooned in warmth, we dream and fly.

Soft whispers glow on dewy grass,
Moments melt as hours pass.
With every giggle, spirits rise,
In sunlit corners, pure surprise.

Beneath the sky's expansive blue,
We gather dreams forged fresh and new.
In laughter's light, we seek and roam,
These sunny spots, our hearts' true home.

Within the rays, the world is kind,
In every glimmer, peace we find.
Here, time slows and worries cease,
In hideaways, we find our peace.

As evening falls, we hold the glow,
In sunlit memories, love will flow.
Each moment shared, a precious beam,
In sunlit hideaways, we dream.

Patterns of Glee in Twilight

As day concedes to night's embrace,
We find our joy in twilight's grace.
The sky adorns with hues of red,
In soft farewell, the sun has shed.

Patterns shift in evening's air,
Filled with laughter, love to share.
Each star ignites a tale of bliss,
In twilight's glow, a gentle kiss.

We dance beneath the stars' soft gleam,
In every twirl, we weave a dream.
Joy's rhythm pulses through the night,
As hearts unite in pure delight.

The world transforms, a canvas bright,
In laughter's tapestry, take flight.
Patterns of glee, a vibrant song,
In twilight's arms, we all belong.

As night unfolds with gentle care,
Our laughter lingers on the air.
In these sweet moments, time stands still,
Patterns of glee our hearts will fill.

Glimmers of Ecstatic Imaginations

In the twilight's gentle glow,
Shadows dance with fireflies,
Whispers weave through the night,
Dreams take flight like butterflies.

Colors burst in vivid streams,
Thoughts unfurl like paper kites,
Laughter rings through the air,
Caught in gauzy starlit nights.

Every sigh a hopeful wish,
Every glance a spark of light,
Heartbeats sync with cosmic rhymes,
Lost in endless, pure delight.

Stars align in twinkling paths,
Leading souls to worlds anew,
In the realm of endless dreams,
Imagination's vibrant hue.

With each breath, a tale unfolds,
Magic swirls in silent spaces,
Glimmers of our wildest hopes,
Infinite in all their graces.

Frolic in Fields of Merry Thoughts

Beneath the sun's warm embrace,
Laughter echoes, sweet and free,
Children dance on emerald grass,
Joyful hearts in happy spree.

Clouds drift by like fluffy dreams,
Tickling toes of daisies bright,
Every moment sparkles gold,
In the glow of pure delight.

Breezes play like gentle hands,
Rustling leaves in softest tune,
Butterflies waltz through the air,
Kissing petals 'neath the moon.

In fields where giggles intertwine,
Stories bloom like fragrant flowers,
Imagination takes its flight,
In these cherished, golden hours.

Together we chase the light,
Through sunbeams, joyfully we roam,
Each thought a thread of fabric spun,
In the tapestry we call home.

Journeys through Giggling Meadows

In meadows bright where laughter sings,
We wander free on whispers soft,
With every step, a new delight,
The world around us lifts us aloft.

Blossoms sway to playful tunes,
While butterflies join in the cheer,
With pockets full of dreams to share,
We cast away both doubt and fear.

Sunshine dapples through the trees,
Painting shadows on our skin,
Life's a canvas colored bright,
Every giggle, fresh begin.

Picnics sprawled on verdant ground,
Stories woven in the breeze,
Tales of wonder, hearts entwined,
Lost in laughter, found with ease.

As twilight dances on the hills,
We gather all our cherished days,
In giggling meadows, love abounds,
Filling life with joyful rays.

The Palette of Bright Beginnings

From dawn's embrace, new colors bloom,
Brushstrokes paint the waking skies,
Horizons gilded with promise sweet,
Each sunrise brings the heart to rise.

Splashes of pink and golden hue,
Canvas stretched where hopes ignite,
Every moment a brush of chance,
Creating visions bold and bright.

With splatters of laughter, stories unfold,
In every hue, a tale whispered,
Life's masterpiece, both wild and free,
In each stroke, a dream configured.

Voices mingle like shades of paint,
Coloring paths we choose to walk,
In this palette of beginnings,
Every heartbeat dares to talk.

As stars emerge in night's embrace,
We sketch our hopes beneath the moon,
In this art of living bright,
New beginnings, like flowers, bloom.

Serenade of Joyful Reveries

In the dawn's gentle light, we play,
Whispers of dreams dance, rich and gay.
Laughter spills like golden rays,
Embracing moments, bright their gaze.

Through fields of color, we shall roam,
Painting our hearts with shades of home.
Every step in joy we find,
Woven tales in heart and mind.

The melody of hearts entwined,
In a symphony of love defined.
Each note a spark, each chord a wing,
Carrying us where hope can sing.

Underneath the starlit sky,
Dreams take flight, and spirits fly.
With every wish that we release,
Together, we find timeless peace.

Let the echoes of our delight,
Fill the world with purest light.
In the reveries, we shall dwell,
For in our hearts, all is well.

Fragments of Cheerful Fantasies

In a tapestry of smiles so bright,
We gather stories, day and night.
Colors blending, dreams awake,
For every joy, a heartbeat's quake.

Through trails of laughter, we will glide,
With open hearts, casting aside.
In each moment, magic flows,
As we weave what friendship knows.

With every whisper of the breeze,
We find our solace, our sweet ease.
Each fragment glimmers, pure and free,
A testament to you and me.

Together wandering, hand in hand,
Creating paths like grains of sand.
In playful circles, we create,
The joyful tunes that celebrate.

May these fragments fill our days,
In cheerful dance, we find our ways.
In every dream that takes its flight,
Together, we embrace the light.

Mosaic of Luminous Aspirations

From shards of hope, we build anew,
Crafting dreams with vibrant hue.
Each desire a shining star,
Guiding us both near and far.

In this mosaic, we find our place,
Woven together with gentle grace.
Every piece a tale to tell,
In life's kaleidoscope, we dwell.

Through laughter and through silent night,
We gather strength with pure delight.
Aspirations rise like dawn,
In unity, we carry on.

With open minds and hearts so clear,
We embrace adventures without fear.
Each luminous thread that we weave,
Becomes a gift we can believe.

As the colors blend and bloom,
We paint away the shades of gloom.
In this mosaic, side by side,
Our hopes and dreams shall never hide.

The Enchantment of Laughter's Embrace

In the cradle of laughter's sound,
Joy surrounds us, peace is found.
With every giggle, spirits rise,
Shimmering dreams beneath the skies.

Through playful whispers, hearts entwine,
In every moment, love will shine.
Each shared chuckle, a gentle song,
In laughter's embrace, we belong.

Bubbles of joy float through the air,
We weave our stories without care.
In these magical tales we share,
Life's sweetest moments, flashes rare.

With friends beside us, warm and true,
Each smile a star, each heart a view.
In the dance of laughter, we find grace,
An enchantment in this sacred space.

Let us cherish each giggling breath,
In laughter's light, we conquer death.
In every embrace that we possess,
Lies the magic of happiness.

Tapestry of Serene Delights

In the soft glow of twilight's embrace,
Whispers of peace dance in the air,
Colorful threads of dreams interlace,
Weaving a tale without a care.

Gentle breezes caress the trees,
As petals flutter, kissed by the light,
Harmony hums on humbling knees,
Inviting hearts to join in the flight.

Morning dew glistens on grassy beds,
Awakening life in quiet delight,
Nature's canvas where beauty spreads,
Illuminates shadows, dispelling the night.

In laughter echoed through the fields,
Each note a joy wrapped in the sun,
The world with its warmth gently yields,
A tapestry where all souls run.

As sunset bows to the evening's reign,
Peace drapes softly like a warm shawl,
In this serene space, free from pain,
Life's simple pleasures inspire us all.

Chasing Starlit Grins

Beneath a vault of shimmering light,
We gather dreams that twinkle bright,
With laughter trailing through the night,
Chasing starlit grins, pure delight.

Constellations guide our playful flight,
As comets trail with a joyful sight,
In tandem we spin, hearts feel so right,
In this cosmic dance under the night.

Each moment captured, a spark on the rise,
Filling our souls with wonder's surprise,
Together we weave, no hidden lies,
Chasing starlit grins, reaching the skies.

Hand in hand, we trace our own maze,
Following fireworks in velvety haze,
Euphoric whispers in youthful praise,
Chasing starlit grins through endless days.

As dawn approaches, the stars start to fade,
But imprints of joy forever displayed,
In the heart's gallery where memories wade,
Chasing starlit grins, our love cascades.

The Comfort of Hopeful Clouds

In the vast blue, where dreams float high,
Hopeful clouds drift and gently sigh,
Wrapped in whispers, they catch the eye,
Offering solace as they glide by.

With every puff, a tale they weave,
Of distant lands and hearts that believe,
In their soft shapes, we dare to perceive,
The comfort they bring, we can receive.

Rainbows born from teardrops of grace,
Paint the sky with a loving embrace,
In the arms of the clouds, find your place,
As whispers of hope time can't erase.

Over meadows, through valleys they roam,
Creating shadows, they establish home,
In their tender folds, our worries comb,
Clouds of comfort where dreams freely comb.

Even as day melts into the night,
Twinkling stars join the clouds in flight,
Together they symbolize our light,
The comfort of clouds, ever so bright.

Gleaming Pathways to Elysium

On paths of gold where the heart can roam,
Whispers of peace beckon us home,
With every step, our spirits comb,
Gleaming pathways to Elysium.

In fields of flowers, colors collide,
Dreams take root where the soul can bide,
Through vibrant meadows, hope is our guide,
On these pathways, joy cannot hide.

Mountains rise with an ancient grace,
Shadows dance in a warm embrace,
Each turn reveals a sacred space,
Gleaming pathways to Elysium trace.

As twilight fades, stars start to gleam,
Leading us forth on our shared dream,
In unity's light, we become a team,
On gleaming pathways, life is supreme.

Together we journey, hand in hand,
Through valleys, over hills, we stand,
In every heartbeat, love is planned,
Gleaming pathways to Elysium so grand.

A Wisp of Laughter in the Breeze

Beneath the trees that sway and dance,
The whispers float, a playful chance.
Children giggle, hearts so free,
Their laughter drifts like leaves from a tree.

The sunbeams kiss the vibrant ground,
In every corner, joy is found.
A soft breeze carries cheerfulness,
With every note, sweet happiness.

Clouds of white, they drift and sigh,
As dreams take flight and hopes comply.
The world awakes with gentle ease,
Embracing life, a wisp of breeze.

Songs of birds fill morning's light,
Creating magic, pure delight.
In laughter's wake, we feel alive,
With every sound, our spirits thrive.

Let laughter be the song we sing,
In every heart, let joy take wing.
A wisp of laughter floats on high,
It's life's sweet gift, a soft goodbye.

The Lightness of Being Spirited Away

In twilight's glow, dreams softly rise,
A sweet escape, beneath the skies.
With whispered wishes, spirits soar,
As starlit pathways open doors.

The tender night sings lullabies,
Details hidden, a sweet surprise.
Each breath we take feels light as air,
In this quiet, we shed our care.

Moments linger, slowly fade,
In this sanctuary, memories made.
A soft embrace, we drift on waves,
As time suspends, our heart behaves.

The moonlight bathes us in its grace,
With every glance, a warm embrace.
In gentle whispers, let us sway,
To the lightness of being, far away.

With every heartbeat, we remain,
Caught in this dance, free from the strain.
Spirited away, we dance tonight,
In the soft glow of the silver light.

Tender Tales of Joyous Reflections

In the quiet morn, soft tales arise,
Whispers of joy, under painted skies.
Memories bloom like flowers rare,
Tender moments, beyond compare.

A gentle breeze stirs dreams anew,
With every heartbeat, love shines through.
Each story told in laughing eyes,
Is painted warm with sweet goodbyes.

The flicker of hope in a child's gaze,
Captured in sunlight's radiant blaze.
Tender tales weaving light and shade,
A tapestry where hearts have laid.

With laughter woven in the air,
Every sorrow fades, leaving care.
In joyous reflections, we find our way,
Cherishing love in bright array.

So gather round, let stories flow,
In every smile, let happiness grow.
Through tender tales, our spirits soar,
In the warmth of love, forevermore.

The Serene Embrace of Glad Tidings

A tranquil morn begins its song,
With gentle breezes, righting wrongs.
Glad tidings bloom in hues so clear,
A sereneness that draws us near.

Each moment cradled in loving light,
Rich with promise, glowing bright.
The heart expands with every cheer,
In kindness shared, we find it here.

Soft sounds of nature weave through time,
A harmony, a gentle rhyme.
In silence held, we count our grace,
Within our hearts, a sacred space.

Let laughter ring where shadows dwell,
In joyful whispers, all is well.
The serene embrace of brighter days,
Wraps us gently in love's soft rays.

So let us gather in the glow,
With every heartbeat, let love flow.
Glad tidings shared, our souls align,
In the embrace of joy divine.

Woven Threads of Blissful Mirth

In the garden where laughter blooms,
Joyful whispers chase away glooms.
Colors weave a vibrant dance,
Every moment, a sweet romance.

Breezes carry soft-spoken dreams,
Flowing gently like silver streams.
Hand in hand, we spin and twine,
Life's a tapestry, truly divine.

Sunlight filters through leafy lace,
Each ray paints a warm embrace.
Together, we dance on tender ground,
In this bliss, true love is found.

Laughter rings through the air we share,
With every smile, we banish despair.
Together, our spirits intertwine,
In this moment, all hearts align.

As the evening stars begin to gleam,
Time stands still; we float, we dream.
Woven threads of bliss, pure and bright,
In this sacred space, all feels right.

Journeys through Radiant Hearts

Across the hills where sunlight wakes,
Hearts embark on paths it makes.
Softly singing, the rivers flow,
Guiding us where wildflowers grow.

Each step taken in joyful haste,
Moments cherished, none to waste.
Together, we brave every climb,
Inside our laughter, we find our rhyme.

Beneath the sky of endless blue,
Every glance feels fresh and new.
Whispers of dreams beneath our feet,
In this journey, our souls meet.

Through valleys low and shadows long,
We carry the echoes of our song.
Every heartbeat a symphony,
As we dance through history.

With radiant hearts, we share our light,
Guiding others through the night.
Journeys of love, vast and grand,
Together creating, hand in hand.

The Elegance of Gleeful Thoughts

In the quiet glance of dawn's first light,
Gleeful thoughts take graceful flight.
Like petals swirling on the breeze,
They dance with joy, aiming to please.

With each idea, a spark ignites,
Painting days in dazzling lights.
Whispers of laughter fill the air,
In elegance, our minds lay bare.

Scribbles on pages, bright and free,
Unlocking doors to creativity.
With every line, a world unfurls,
Gleeful thoughts, a gift that swirls.

Moments cherished, gleefully bright,
Every notion shines in delight.
Through the corridors of our dreams,
The elegance sparkles and gleams.

As twilight wraps the day in grace,
Gleeful thoughts find their rightful place.
In the heart's garden, they take root,
Blossoming wildly, a sweet pursuit.

Dances Beneath a Smiling Moon

Underneath the moon's soft glow,
Laughter echoes, spirits flow.
Stars above twinkle with glee,
In this moment, wild and free.

The night whispers secrets untold,
As we sway, our dreams unfold.
With every step, we cast aside,
Fears and worries that abide.

Embraced by shadows, our hearts ignite,
In the stillness, we find our light.
Dancing close, we share our fears,
Each movement crafted through the years.

Moonbeams fall like softest lace,
In their shimmer, we find our place.
Together, we twirl, let our souls soar,
The world forgotten—who could ask for more?

As dawn approaches, the stars fade out,
Yet echoes of joy are what we shout.
Beneath the moon's lingering embrace,
We find solace, our timeless space.

The Bright Flame of Playful Yearnings

In gardens where the laughter grows,
Children dance, with joy it flows.
Kites are soaring, hearts take flight,
Each moment sparkles, pure delight.

Whispers of dreams in gentle air,
Stories of wonder, beyond compare.
Balloons rise high to touch the sun,
In the realm of play, we find our fun.

The world is bright with colors bold,
In our hearts, the treasures unfold.
Chasing shadows, we run and spin,
With laughter echoing deep within.

The sun sets low, yet spirits soar,
In every heartbeat, we explore.
The flame of play will never wane,
In every joy, we dance again.

Shimmering Threads of Lively Enchantment

A tapestry of dreams we weave,
In every stitch, our hearts believe.
Colors dancing, side by side,
In this magic, we take our ride.

The moonlight whispers, soft and bright,
Guiding us through the velvet night.
With every twinkle, a story blooms,
In the stillness, joy resumes.

The stars above sing songs of old,
In their glow, our hopes unfold.
Through shimmering threads, new paths we find,
Lively enchantment, heart and mind.

As dawn arrives, the colors blend,
In every corner, dreams ascend.
With laughter woven in the air,
Together, we go anywhere.

Clouds of Light and Laughter

Fluffy clouds drift across the sky,
Filled with giggles, they float by.
Here and there, they twist and turn,
In their shadows, the children learn.

Sunny rays poke through the fluff,
Chasing worries away, enough!
Joyful echoes ring in the breeze,
As laughter dances among the trees.

With every giggle, spirits rise,
Clouds of light become our prize.
Drifting freely, hearts entwined,
In this haven, hope defined.

In the tapestry of day and night,
We find the beauty in pure light.
With laughter, love, and dreams so bright,
Clouds of joy, our endless flight.

Lullabies of a Cheerful Dawn

As night surrenders to morning's glow,
Soft lullabies begin to flow.
The sun peeks 'round the sleepy trees,
Whispering warmth upon the breeze.

Birds awaken, singing clear,
Carrying melodies for all to hear.
In a world kissed by golden hues,
Every heart sings its own news.

A gentle touch from nature's hand,
Unfolding beauty across the land.
With every breath, we start anew,
In the dawn's embrace, the world feels true.

The cheerful hum of life abounds,
In this moment, joy surrounds.
Through lullabies, our hearts respond,
To the magic of this cheerful dawn.